Eyes of Dew

Eyes of Dew

◻

Poems by
Chonggi Mah

◻

Translated by
Brother Anthony of Taizé

◻

KOREAN VOICES SERIES: VOLUME 11

WHITE PINE PRESS / BUFFALO, NEW YORK

The translation and publication of this book was made possible by the generous support of the Korea Literature Translation Institute and the Sunshik Min Endowment for the Advancement of Korean Literature at the Korea Institute, Harvard University, and with public funds from the New York State Council on the Arts, a State Agency.

Korean Voices Series: Volume 11

First Edition.

Cover art by Lena Mah.

10-digit ISBN: 1-893996-79-4
13-digit ISBN: 978-1-83996-79-3

Printed and bound in the United States of America.

Library of Congress Control Number: 2006923282

White Pine Press
P.O. Box 236
Buffalo, New York 14201
www.whitepine.org

Contents

TRANSLATOR'S PREFACE

Chonggi Mah was born in Tokyo, Japan, on January 17, 1939. His father, Mah Haesong, worked as a literary journalist in Japan and served as one of the earlier editors of a highly reputed Japanese literary magazine, *Bungeishunju*. He is still revered in Korea as a major writer of children's literature. His mother, Park Oesôn, was famed as one of the first Korean ballet dancers, touring extensively in Japan and Korea. Later she became the head of the first dance department in Korea, at Ewha Womens University. In 1944, before the end of the war, the family returned to Korea and the future poet began his schooling there. He witnessed scenes of horror when the North Korean army occupied Seoul at the start of the Korean War in June 1950; his family later fled further south and returned to Seoul at the end of the war in 1953. He began to write while only a child and thought at first of studying humanities at university, but finally he chose instead to study medicine at Seoul's Yonsei University, on his parents' advice.

During his pre-med studies at Yonsei, he joined a literary circle under the guidance of the poet Park Tu-jin and published poems in the university newspaper. Park Tu-jin recommended his poems to the major literary review *Hyôndae munhak*, where they were published in 1959 and 1960, establishing him as a recognized poet. He immediately published a collection of his youthful poems, *Quiet Triumph (Choyonghan kaesôn)* that received the first annual Yonsei Literary Award in 1961. After graduating in 1963, he did his military service in the Air Force as a doctor. In

1965 he signed a petition in which writers living in Seoul protested against the upcoming Korean-Japanese summit. This was against military law; he was arrested, detained for ten days and tortured during questioning. Released, he continued his studies and military service until 1966.

As soon as he received his honorable discharge from the air force, he left for the United States. Once he had completed his medical training, including an internship and radiology residency at the Ohio State University hospital, he was certified by the American Board of Radiology. He moved to Toledo, Ohio, in 1971 and there Chonggi Mah was appointed assistant professor in the department of radiology and pediatrics. From that moment on, he set out on a double career. His work in the medical field was situated almost entirely in the United States, while his poetry was all written in Korean and published in Korea. He soon became a well-known poet in his native country, but although English translations of some of his poems have been published in anthologies in the United States, he remains virtually unknown there as a poet.

In 1968 and 1972, two collections of poems were published with works by Hwang Tong-Kyu, Kim Yông-T'ae, and Chonggi Mah, *Well-Tempered Clavier (P'yônggyunyul)* and *Well-Tempered Clavier 2 (P'yônggyunyul 2)*. In 1976 he published a collection of poems, *Frontier Flowers (Pyônkyông ûi kkot)* which received the 3rd Korean Literary Writers' Award. In the meantime, living in the United States, he came to play a leading role in the local Korean community and also in the medical society of the State of Ohio. He received the best professor award from the graduating class of 1975 at the medical school where he taught. In 1980 his collection *Invisible Land of Love (An poinûn sarang ûi nara)* was published in Seoul and in 1982 he published a selection of already published poems, *And an Age of Peace (Kûrigo p'yônghwahan sidaega)*. In 1986 appeared *How Should Living Together Be Only for Reeds? (Moyôsô sanûn kôsi ôdi kaltaedulppunirya)*, which was awarded the first Korean-American Literary Award. He played a leading role in establishing the Korean Catholic community in Toledo, Ohio. For several years he served as President of the Toledo Radiological Associates (TRA), comprised of over thirty radiologists. In 1991 he published *The Color of That Country's Sky (Kû nara hanûlpit)*. In 1994, his younger brother was killed in a shooting incident, a tragic loss mentioned in a number of his poems.

In 1997 he published *Eyes of Dew (Isûl ûi nun)*, which earned him both the P'yônun Literary Award and the Isan Literary Award, two of Korea's most important literary prizes. In 1999, to mark his sixtieth birthday a volume of his collected poems *Collected Poems of Chonggi Mah (Ma Chonggi sijônchip)*, over 500 pages in length, and a collection of critical essays inspired by his work *Reading Chonggi Mah in Depth (Ma Chonggi kip'iilki)* were published. In the same year, he received the honor of being inducted as a fellow of the American College of Radiology, the most respected title possible for a radiologist to receive. He moved to Florida on retiring from teaching and medical practice in 2002. In that year he published *In the Birds' Dreams Trees are Fragrant (Saedul ûi kkum esônûn namu naemsaega nanda)* which received the East-West Literary Award. Since his retirement from teaching and medical practice, he has divided his time between Florida and Korea. In Korea, he regularly lectures on 'literature and medicine' as a visiting professor in the medical school of Yonsei University, his Alma Mater.

From this biography, it is clear that Chonggi Mah's life has followed a double course, medicine and poetry. The influence of his parents was very important in the early stages. His father loved reading, and as a dancer his mother embodied the notion of artistic beauty. Even in the days of intense poverty during and after the Korean War, his parents encouraged him to learn about music and the visual arts. Some of his earliest poems and essays were inspired by paintings and music by famous artists. Yet it took something more to turn him into the poet he has become. That proved to be the experiences he underwent as a medical student then as a doctor. As he has written,

"I had to cut into, dissect and touch dead bodies, feel every part of the human body with my eyes, hands and heart. That made me aware of life and death and reflect how I should live. I came to realize that writing and reading poems had become almost my sole consolation, an indispensable condition for my real life. Poetry offered the sole means to identify myself as I went through hard times as an intern in a foreign land.

"I arrived in the United States penniless, on a ticket sent by a hospital in a quiet Mid-West city. The first year I spent there, speaking poor English, working as an inexperienced doctor unfamiliar with the culture of this new land, was the longest year of my life, and the hardest. It proved to be critical as a new beginning in my career as a writer.

"My apartment was only a ten minutes' walk away, yet for one whole month I never had the time to go there. A hundred and fifty patients died before my eyes; I watched as they lay poised between life and death, groaning in pain, longing to live. I had to watch so many of them breathe their last, and invariably tears would run down their cheeks. I sometimes made friends with a patient to whom I could open myself freely. But when such friends died, there almost always had to be an autopsy. In those days, the autopsy rate was nearly eighty percent, incomparably higher than in Korea, and watching those autopsies was a great torment. The pathologists used power saws to cut through the skulls, then removed the brains of friends who had, only a few days before, been talking about politics or love. Day after day, they cut open the corpses of my friends, removed heart, lungs, liver, kidneys, identified the cause of death, washed away the blood, and all the time I strove to remain calm as if I were a fearless doctor. To cope with my sense of pain, sorrow and emptiness, whenever I had time I would try to write a poem that would function as a sedative, plunging into the nostalgic world of my mother tongue.

"Even after that internship, it was as if I were fated to observe autopsies, for as a resident in the radiology department, I had to attend autopsies for another two years, comparing the results of the autopsies with the radiological diagnoses. In contrast, there were times when I was able to restore a child to health who had been at death's door, and the child threw himself into my arms in gratitude. I helped deliver some two hundred babies, cutting their umbilical cords, hearing their newborn cries of life. My whole body thrilled with a sense of the beauty, the miracle of life. I strove hard to transcribe in my poems that kind of excitement.

"Practicing medicine, I wavered between peaks of joy and the depths of fear and despair. I know now that I could never have become a true poet in my own country if I had not lived for many years elsewhere, with a deep sense of loneliness, constantly witnessing the death of friends and obliged to see their internal organs, their blood. Why did I go on writing? Because when I was mentally and physically in deepest darkness in a foreign country, it proved to be my only consolation. Because poetry served as a consolation, it expressed my true feelings, my true heart. If a heart is not true, how can it offer comfort to others? I have always tried to be honest and truthful in my poetry.

"All who write poetry know what a blessing it is when someone listens in full accord to the song of our heart and sings together with us. But at the outset, no one can write poetry to obtain that happiness. Poetry, I believe, is a matter of individual experience, it is a kind of private muttering. If poetry is merely a highbrow game, no matter how expensive a perfume it wears it will never be able to compete with computer games, and it will be doomed to a slow extinction. If poetry becomes a kind of propaganda and focuses only on issues of social justice, it cannot compete with conventional shouted slogans, having only the power of angry manifestoes. Probably because I have lived for so long in the stink of real blood, I feel instinctively suspicious of the 'sweat and blood' so often mentioned with that kind of poetry.

"Since I have always believed that literature is a matter of sharing, I hope that it will continue to be loved by many in this world so full of constant wars and slaughter. Having spent much of my life as a doctor, I have always been in close touch with life. Naturally, then, the main topic of my poetry has been life. Human life is always searching for hope and love; I have written poems and accepted the trivial pains I suffered as I did so.

"I agree with those who say that every life, despite outward appearances, bears a similarly heavy burden. But while agreeing that we all have to bear heavy burdens, I also recall that the pain caused by a slightly crooked back is almost a hallmark of love. Accepting that, I continue my pilgrimage through this world in search of love."

There is little to be added to that. Certainly, the early poems in which Chonggi Mah writes directly about his experiences as a medical student and a young doctor are almost unique in modern world literature, powerful and shattering reminders of what most doctors are never able to mention, either to family or friends, and certainly not to their patients. Yet without passing through that dark valley, no practice of medicine would be possible, and unless the darkness is recognized and faced up to, the quality of compassion would be unable to develop. Such poems have a very special power.

Yet most of Chonggi Mah's verse is not about being a doctor. Many poems are celebrations of love, or intimations of the difficulty and pain of loving. He does not burden us with details about who the significant persons might be in his poems and life; instead, he opens doors to the many kinds of memory locked within each reader. Love is, after all, often more marked by loneliness than fulfillment. The solitude he evokes is not only that of the foreigner and the doctor, it is the fundamental human condition that we so often wish to avoid. Many poems express aspects of the natural world, landscapes, moments of remembered experience that hold suggestions of hidden meaning. Only rarely does he make explicit mention of themes related to Christian faith, yet we never forget that he was baptized with the name Lawrence in 1959, when he was twenty and in freshman year in medical school, studying anatomy. Lawrence was a Roman martyr, reputed to have been burned to death very slowly. He is synonymous with pain endured heroically.

I am grateful to the poet Kim Kwang-Kyu for introducing me to Chonggi Mah and suggesting that I translate some of his poems, that I might otherwise never have discovered. I am deeply grateful to Dr. Mah for the hours he has spent going through my draft translations, checking them, and for his patience as we sat together reflecting on what changes and improvements should be made. This is the first time that I have translated a Korean poet whose English is good enough to make it possible for us to work together on the final versions; it has been a pleasure and a great privilege. I hope that these translations may enable Dr. Mah to be recognized at last as a poet in the country where most of his poems were written, but where he is almost only known for his medical work. He refers with special depth of feeling to William Carlos Williams because he, too, was a doctor-poet; this combination clearly yields very special fruit, as I hope this volume shows.

—Brother Anthony

Note: In the text above, the poet is referred to in Western style as Chonggi Mah since that is how he is always known in the United States, where he has lived for so long, but all the other Korean names are printed in conventional Korean style, with the family name first.

from

Quiet Triumph

(1960)

Anatomy Lab II

Why, just look at that child,
that little girl, her eyes tightly shut,
smiling, her breast wrapped in flowery white.

We cannot cry, even silently,
for this is no grave.

You set out to live a whole lifetime,
but you finally, quickly wearied of all.

Now, you're here gazing up at the white ceiling,
and your flesh is bleached pale.

The lads who used to tease you once
have scattered now, one after another, seeming lonely;
speak up, little girl, too shy to open your eyes.

Once you used to roam the hills
nibbling flowers, spitting colored spittle;
you used to laugh simply
at that smell, the smell of falling sunshine.

We hold our breath,
extend our two hands.

Why, just look at that child.
Listen to her fragrant breathing,
still smiling there with her dimpled cheeks,
teaching us with our cold palms
the warm art of parting.

Quiet Prayers

I.

Rapture and warmth are displayed when at last
we bare our faces' naked expressions.

Taking up a skull with one hand
I sniff the faint fragrance of my own face.

Yesterday laughing, gloom all forgotten,
my laughing face, friends' faces,
each such a delicate, porcelain sculpture.

Every time I slice muscle from muscle
I hear the sound of the sea one summer's evening,
a beautiful voice I still recall.

How relieved this girl must feel now
as I labor to tear away
her dirty clothing, scattered around her.

2.

I hope the clothes I'm so fondly wearing
will slowly, without my realizing, turn into old rags.

When the time comes, I hope I can gladly prepare new clothes
then go flying off, lightly flapping my arms.

I hope I'll enjoy a mysterious happiness – flying,
rising, flying away on a lengthy journey.

Like this girl lying, eyes closed, on the dissecting table,
let me be used, let me begin.

Psychiatric Ward

One rainy autumn afternoon
the psychiatric ward stands there.
It's spring, after spring comes winter and after winter, burglars come.
How old am I? Five hundred and two. I have twenty-one wives.

One strongly built youth stands there;
he broke down while studying for the bar exam.
One dying tree laughs.
Well, with Wagner's style the question, I can only laugh.
Don't you think?

In every corner of the psychiatric ward
primeval moss grows.
Narcissus' watery mirror gleams,
drenched by the rain.

All have come back now.
Abstracted fully, an art student
who produced abstraction after abstraction,
now remains unwearied
after a whole day spent
staring at a white page—
and this clown in a gown
only grows sad at rain falling.
Now they are all awake.

Love Song IV

One day, while you suddenly
turn into a young flower of the fields
and stand here in front of this ocean,

I'll set out on a journey,
seized with the dizziness that comes
at the end of a long-lasting high fever.

My blissful sister,
lying stretched flat
on the shores of oblivion.

The crowds ebbing away
take no note of you.

After all, love was
such a trifling thing!

Deathbed

When the light goes out in the westward sickroom,
the dark shadow of winter
passes beyond the low hills

and the chill bricks of the autopsy room
ring to the sound of a skull being sawed,
it's no finale.

I first learned about
natural life in anatomy class.
That's when the cold came.

On my lonely, youthful bed
I often found myself sentenced to death.
The dazzling vertigo of the remaining hours.
Don't you see? The solitary deathbed
of the tall guy who gave up.
Don't you see? This is no finale.

Memorandum II

Und doch ist Einer, welcher dieses Fallen
unendlich sanft in seinen Händen hält.
—Ranier Maria Rilke

I.

The exhumation takes place
one dull winter's day.

He's been dead ten years,
lying on one side, short of breath
and insensitive history
is growing downward with positive geotropism.

His heart was big,
his skull is light.
We learn why his tears are cold.

Fine tree roots doze
in eye-sockets,
between toe-bones,

while sunsets left behind in deep sleep
and unfamiliar winds striking bare flesh
all grow downward with positive geotropism.

You, once a wanderer, now
are changed into a loam that cherishes flower-seeds.

2.

As I made my way home after treating a 19-year-old driver for syphilis, winter had arrived downtown and was undressing. That driver giggled as he undressed. Where shall I get off? Somewhere near Kwanghwa-mun, or Anguk-dong, or Donhwa-mun? A dead friend suddenly hails me, waving a hand.

On my way home after giving advice to a senior officer who claimed he could not sleep from a sense of inferiority, scratching my head then prescribing more medicine, winter has settled in and snow settles on my empty palm. Petals melting on my empty palm—tell me, where shall I get off?

Note: The epigraph is from the poem "Herbst" [Autumn]:
    And yet there is One who holds this falling
    infinitely gently in his hands.

Lecture Room Number Three

I.

In the third year of medical school, one bright, sunny autumn afternoon, sitting at an ancient desk some twenty or thirty years old, I was listening to an obstetrics lecture in lecture room number three, on the second floor. The baby was just emerging from the mother's pelvis, its head bent, while the mother was enduring with her whole being the pain of expanding to a ten-centimeter diameter. But with the birth of a living being more precious than pain, finally wrapping itself in its mother's pain the baby burst out crying. That lecture room, in which I attended classes, was a place where a thousand students had preceded me over many years. After concentrating on the lecture for a while, I leaned my head against the wall. The wall took away all my anxieties, it delayed all kinds of difficult challenges for me. Suddenly I realized that behind the wall was the dissection lab, with its corpses laid out side by side. There the friends of my future lay, who had taught me to drink, then to go back to poetry-writing and to faith.

2.

Plaster had peeled from the ceiling, suggesting a kind of sculpture, and there swarms of flies were disgorging the anxieties filling the human flesh they had ingested. But look—one, two, and there another—golden flashes of sunlight dancing! That must be those girls again.

Behind the classroom, outside the window was an alley as complex as our nervous system, running between hovels with roofs made of old army tents. Looking down, it was those girls again. Few customers come in the daytime, so when they wake up from their morning doze, they always do the same, without bothering to wash. A broken mirror in the hand of some woman whose marriage broke down reflects sunlight into the classroom. "Come on down! Come on down! I'll do it for free!" They were promising to teach us the songs in praise of youth they learned from their frequent night-time customers. "Come on down! Come on down!"

Watching those magic sunlight parties, our eyes gleamed and we began to feel refreshed, like when listening to Mozart's Clarinet Concerto. Come on down! Come on down! For free! We were still incapable of listening to music with quiet minds, like listening to people talking.

3.

The obstetrics class ended after we had learned how best to sleep in fetal position while observing a mother in a difficult labor with the baby in the wrong position. As the class ended, it began to rain. At the dismal sound of rain, the "come on down" girls who had been so cheerful withdrew into their dream palaces, while from below the window on that side a heart-rending song could be heard. It was coming from the single-storied pathology department's autopsy room. An oldish country-woman, both hands against the red brick wall, was calling: "Sun-a, Sun-a," and beating at the wall.

But we in lecture room number three had been hearing that kind of song once or twice a day for weeks past. At first, it had constricted my throat, then later provided food for thought; once past that, I had slowly grown deaf and lost interest, but now I had reached a point where my ears had opened and it sounded like music—the kind of music you might hear for example in the steppes of Central Asia. With rain falling, autumn advancing, and raindrop beads hanging from every leaf, I suddenly thought of the Sun-a of my childhood days. 'Sun-a, Sun-a, let's you and I live together; we'll spend every day laughing.' As I groped for words, there was only one pretty Sun-a in all the world as far as I was concerned. "*Aigu, aigu,* poor little Sun-a," the mother's hoarse voice was feeble but the weeping emerged shaking from somewhere between her long, rain-soaked hair and her white cotton skirt.

Her innocent child had died ahead of her, and on the slab in the autopsy room a senior doctor was sawing open Sun-a's chest and taking out her lungs and heart. Watery blood seeping out reminded me of the time when she was still alive.

4.

Once the lecture was over, I was going to have to leave lecture room number three, carrying my book-bag. First, I would have to give an SM injection to a tubercular friend confined to his tiny room, then meet a girl who had been a friend since childhood, but was setting off for a new continent she had discovered. That girl friend, who had been extremely pretty and attractive as a child, had now, a few years later, gone way ahead of me and become quite dazzling.

I was thinking I would have to empty my pockets and buy a plastic umbrella, but could not help hesitating at the thought that a plastic umbrella would not suit her. But since I had recently gotten into the habit of wavering where she was concerned, I reflected that a plastic umbrella suited me better.

A sudden transmigration! In lecture room number three, a baby had just been born, and the "come on down" girls, having eaten their fill, burst into a popular song about the height of youth, while the corpses prayed toward the ceiling as if mocking the world—and the woman against the wall of the autopsy room is arriving at the finale of her version of "'Death and the Maiden." Just then, sudden transmigration!

After hesitating again for a while, first I felt an aching hunger rather than transmigration. For that was the time of the scientific age developing artificial satellites. Carrying my book-bag, I seized a plastic umbrella, reluctant as I was, then turned off the street into a *makkolli* den. It was like my own lecture room . . .

5.

The friend waiting in his tiny room will soon be setting out on a renewed fresh youth, while the prayer of the girl devoted to a new continent is to wake up from the dream she once shared with me and set out on her journey. Still, she seems to regret something, and is delaying a little before leaving.

"Sorry, you've been waiting a long time." The students were roasting sizzling tripe in lecture room number three. Now outside it's raining hard enough to wash the road away. For my own tranquility too the road needs to be blocked briefly. I can't walk any further. I'll try again once this rain is past. "Sorry, you've been waiting a long time."

from
Well-Tempered Clavier
(1968)

Winter's Tale I

How did winter come?
Night falls early across empty gardens and
the river that was so bright falls silent,
a layer of frost covering its cheeks.

I was on my way to Uijôngbu,
with snow falling unexpectedly
and in the late-night bus
the Revelation of Saint John shaking,
then, under the night's falling snow, look—
an inscription on a passing tombstone.

Quiet tears course down each of the wrinkles
on the face of an old man dying
and winter remains alone
at the speed of those same tears.

Memorandum III

Ah, after you had buried your blood—your child—in frozen ground, you wrapped clay from beneath the fields in a cloth that by day you caressed and by night hugged and fed with your milk. That earth lay sprinkled each day on your white breasts, in the iron-doored sickroom, maternal love here labeled disease.

Once I fall into nightmare-filled sleep at the end of prolonged sleep-lessness, in my dreams I meet dead friends and we rejoice, gulp cold liquor together in back-alley bars, then when I awake, the excruciating hangover that lingers on, the dreary high-heaped snowdrifts, and even when I went back to Inch'ŏn several years after, the ocean approached me and said: Friend, arrive at a silent hour and quietly melt.

Now a state of emergency covers the frozen land, and when I enter my boarding house in tall military boots, the sound of a night train rattles against the cold floor; one by one many of the dead I have watched over begin to gather. Body temperature dropping all night long. When morning dawns, earth suddenly remains on my breast, ample peace on my hands.

Love Song IX

I.

I spend my life
saying farewell.

Dead friends come quietly by,
in a spring day's rain
whispering in my ear,
for dying and living is like a sound of water.

Is it so? The spring day is already dark
and from those friends I'm learning in secret
the end of hollow laughter.

2.

Early one dark morning in May during my medical school days, after
I had spent the night in the anatomy lab with its lined-up corpses, I
found myself confessing my innocent love, under dim light-bulbs amidst
whispering corpses; we were wearing gowns stained with human flesh.

Before one year was over, the corpses had crumbled away and our love
had broken up, but as I grew older without growing up, I advanced,
improving my skills of indoor wandering, indoor stillness. There was
something I had to think about as I stood far off, a young patient who
had said she wanted to drink a cup of tea, and by the next day had
turned into a nicely softened sound.

3.

If I saw a friend,
I asked

about the idly walking figure seen from behind,
the meaning of the evening exhausted at the end of one whole day.

In the night, awakened by chance,
I asked
about the empty list I own,
the desolate night's calling voice,
that long awaited encounter
when our inner wishes
are sunk deep under water.

Love Song X

I.

One evening boarding in such an awkward-feeling town, I decided to watch a Walt Disney cartoon. The boarding house was so run-down I was being thoroughly robbed, so the cinema with its stove burning was just the thing. While I too became a grasshopper in that technicolor world, my feet froze outside as I went then returned alone under endlessly falling snow.

2.

Wandering round the library, I idly selected a book on respiratory diseases; on the front page was the signature of R. K. Alexandria and in ink: —Boston, Massachusetts, August 2, 1879. The weather on August 2, 1879, must have been hazy. I study the hazy writing, the marks left by a physician now in his grave, Dr. Alexandria. I write 1966 inside my book; I too will become a fine physician.

3.

Once I had a fine house with a porch, I was going to install a classy doorbell and prepare to welcome lonely friends. Writing letters on blue airmail forms, I would love the winter; after donning rimless glasses and growing a little beard, I'd prepare to read Hesse's *Augustus* in a gentle, quiet voice. Now you have come to know me, to know at most only six months of conversation left, six months of love, six months of this world, six months of evenings, and remaining for me six months of heartbreak, six months of tears.

Painting by Rouault

I looked and saw—
standing before my first original Rouault—
adolescence remaining in a corner of Seoul,
classical retinal cells.
I looked and saw—
dust on the painting,
silence on the dust,
love of no use to my homeland.
If dying and living are so close,
I would ascribe my sorrow to vainglory,
even if that voice rang clearly in my ear.
I looked and saw—
all my domains accumulated since childhood,
all my belongings had gone without trace.

Learning to be a doctor

—for Hans Carossa

I confess:
though I'm thirty now, I frequently dream
of anxious exams and writing answers.
No sign of me ever dying for others,
stirring up the crowds of history
and firing the gun of revolution,
nor even the solitude of an ascetic
practicing my exalted religion.

I confess:
I sat at my study desk engrossed
in a novel,
regretting a night spent drinking.
In my study days
life becomes more difficult day by day
despite making pulses beat with a battery
despite people having nuclear physics embedded in their abdomens.

I confess:
there's a western-style grave at the back of a park,
flowers wilting before that grave,
your wilting world.

Dance I

—for Pouline Koner

I too once experienced a love
like your dancing.
Once when one gesture
remained deep in my heart
so that I bowed my head beneath its weight—
was it spring? Was it autumn?
With the strained expression of
the artist you revered
I too climbed the steps
to visit you.
I loved without words of greeting,
like your motionless dance,
silent music
yet as fulfilling as your dance.

from

Korea in the Caribbean Sea

(1972)

Case Report I

Born in Louisville, Kentucky, age 29,
white, male, unmarried,
death confirmed: November 3, 1966.

While you were alive,
while you were talking and laughing
I was dressed in a large gown
dreaming of *kimchi.*
While you were alive,
while you were showing off the photo of your blonde sweetheart,
I was dreaming of my mother.
When you died,
dawn was standing outside the sixth-floor window bidding farewell
while I signed your death certificate
after a single minute's examination.
Life passed unknown
and was simply rendered up, and now
in the hospital garden where the nightlong rain has stopped
stands one lustrous tree,
and turning suddenly, there you are.

Case Report II

Old Mrs. Brashire from the house next door used to sit in her rattan chair telling stories of emigrating to America. That lonely tone of voice, despite the way the wisdom gained from a New York City education shone in her glasses. No successful progeny beside her, picture frames from the past shining in her second-floor room.

Still the same when the hospital warned she was dying. While colorful cards and arrangements of mail-order flowers shone bright in the setting sun, no visitors came for her. You were my patient, this foreign doctor. I see the solitude of a vast country. On the iron table of the autopsy room, though I cut through the skull, peel the skin from the face, extract the viscera, I see for myself your solitude with its quietly closed mouth.

I know all my patients very well. I hear the dark confessions in the wards, hear the sound of last wishes and death approaching. So when death comes, slowly or abruptly, I break apart the flesh, diagnose the disease, then laying my long silence in the blank space of the completely empty abdominal cavity, I shut the door.

My dear! Attractive, loveable dear! I cannot remember your eyes by the blood that once gave strength to the limbs of the dead. One day from our abdominal cavities, too, nameless wild flowers will grow, life will spring up again transformed, and then gaining control over this present world's gales we shall see again. We shall meet in the mountain valley stream, my dear.

Rumor from the Past

Wind, you really give up so easily.
One evening a little while back you roared
knocking, knocking at the windows and the next day
the whole world was piled with fallen leaves
as the wind waved an elderly hand
from that lofty sky above.
Your voice is a chill in the spine,
the monotonous dream of a winter tree sleeping.

Really, you endure so easily.
Breathing in unseen places,
light snow falling quite without warning
your skin the back surface of deepest winter,
something that cannot be real,
wind, that I sometimes feel happened in the past.

Case Report V

I.

You died; it was not only because of my misdiagnosis, but when you left ward twelve on your way to the funeral parlor I had neither the energy nor the courage to go back home. Forgive me.

Really, the misdiagnosis was me becoming a doctor, the proof being the plentiful errors I made at all those exams in high school, while for your death there will only be a headstone.

In the alley where you were born, or in some dream, if you come across someone living remorsefully, forgive them. Unforgiven remorse scorches the heart. But night comes more quickly than contrition.

2.

When I pass the cemetery at dawn
there is always a smell of mint.
The rectangular window emitting that minty smell
and the dawn outside that window
need practice looking in.
The reality of one individual's ionization
without ceiling or floor or corners.
Raising that fresh lively body
when evening falls, you will witness
me washing my hands
and coming in quest of your fingerprints.

Case Report VI

—for little Anne Sanders

Until I became the father of a child, a patient was just a patient, old or child alike; until I became a father, I treated them like a machine, responding with unseen fury to their tears; until I became the father of a pretty child growing day by day, a flower of empathy never once came budding in my eyes.

After a thick needle had been inserted into your breastbone and you had been diagnosed with a disease that left you not long to live, I avoided your sickroom; when you waved your hand with feverish cheeks I once again became a bewildered wanderer. Then on the day when you were dying in my arms, I gazed at you, so pretty in life. Ah, now I'm budding with pain; your pain has become a sound of water that whispers night and day.

Don't resent, child. Don't resent that mob of philosophers who claim that once someone dies anywhere in the world, that's the end of it. You are kinder than they are. The older someone grows, the greater the amnesia, it seems, and eyes that see only what is visible grow dim. They are laughing, child, but after you died you showed me clearly—alive or dead, there is no parting.

Toys

All my childhood toys
were reduced to trash
by the end of the Second World War,
and all through the Korean War
I survived on pumpkin gruel,
messing about in the mud
with the clouds in the summer sky
that I gazed up at hungrily.

My child!
Little child greeting his father
as he comes back home with shoulders drooping:
Nowadays your bright smile
is my only toy and
I'm the empty field,
with your toy rolling around.

An empty field
that finds it hard to get to sleep
even after you have fallen asleep.

Two Kinds of Daily Life

At the end of an evening in unfamiliar surroundings
I fill a coffee cup
with music by Bach and drink.

Having been several years here in the West,
an immense distance
senses the true taste of things.

Overcoming that distance,
paddy fields parched by drought, their skin peeling
in some remote corner of Chôlla province
leap from the page of an old newspaper, come alive
and suddenly turn into my brother.

Brother, dead or alive,
your shadow is long and thin.
Hastily stuffing that unchanging shadow
into a pocket
I attend a party beneath high ceilings.

At night
I draw out the crumpled shadow
and wave it
like a forgotten flag.

At present I am uncomfortably aware
of that bulky, voluminous pocket
and my shadow's music.

In a Bathhouse

Water washes water clean.
Gentle water
scrubs at hardened water.
I am scrubbing
at your soft body.

Our love too was water
once,
the indentations of flesh
seen in the mirror,
the not so clearly seen solitudes.

Emerging into an alley in Myôngryun-dong
when bathing was over
on a Sunday afternoon at the end of a shower
like a rainbow,
like a five-colored rainbow,
like a light, clean giddiness.

Water washes water clean.
Transparent water
scrubs
at less than transparent water.

Time past and now,
the gurgling of bath water,
my entire body,
all turn back into water, cold and transparent,
early winter rain falling
somewhere in Myôngryun-dong.

Our love too was water
once,
the warmth still lingering
in the solid flesh.

After Death III

—to my father

Your smile
is an inorganic substance—
not consumed when burned
completely unchanged
though buried deep,
changing into eternity's music
deeply, intensely performed still.

Your smile
is what lies beyond my window.
Changing when I look out
into grass or a tree,
a breeze, fog, the sky,
your smile
is the landscape enclosing me
wherever I go.

And an Age of Peace

And an age of peace comes.
A drumbeat from an earlier age booms out,
the sound of a gong fills the universe,
brothers stand shoulder to shoulder and weep.
Ancestors who used the same language for many millennia
arise, brushing off the clinging earth.
In sea and on dry land, on hills in all directions
the spirits of those who lost their lives, blind and deaf
shout in triumph, mad once again.
A huge premonition overwhelms the land
and to the vibrations of an unaccustomed mass of flowers
the center of the peninsula collapses swooning.

Born and brought up abroad, I
spent my adolescence in the old country
and have now come back to a foreign land.
The memories that remain of my adolescence's high summer
are corpses killed by guns and spears,
a thousand, ten thousand, a million corpses
dead, rotting, dragged from wells,
piled up like firewood, burned, charred.
Now even twenty years later, at dawn and in dreams
my adolescence falls into a well
where all its flesh creeps
at the low-pitched chorus of the evil doers.

Study a globe for just one night;
if you sound it out, compute again,
you will see how shameful is the eye of greed
in this beautiful land small as a baby's fingernail.
Look again, ask again.
Count on your fingers the nations
more wretched than ours,
more pitiful than ours.

Though I beat my breast, the fault is mine.
The wretchedness is all our fault.

Waking from some early morning nightmare
I suddenly feel traces of tears.
Who can block the fall of every snowflake?

Dead bodies lie strewn all across the realm;
gathering yellow and red phosphorus from their bones and eyes
I will kindle the millions of candles
that keep going out then being lit anew—
and times of peace will come.
The lands of Koguryô and the plains of Parhae
given away out of kindness of heart,
and the DMZ made into a national park—
I can see the rabbits running across that park.

from

Frontier Flowers

(1976)

A Blind Man's Eyes

—at a Giacometti exhibition

You are dead
but your love remains.
Your solitude alone remains,
the most enduring aspect of love.
Exploring the back-alleys of that solitude
the blind man thinks
with unseen eyes
and you weep
with an unseen body.
Then all we who once collapsed
raise our heads again,
help one another up
in another direction. We walk out.

Psychiatric Ward II

We meet
walking down the path of an oesophagus
constricted after drinking caustic soda
to cleanse the body's inner parts.

We meet
beginning with the early morning baptism
of the fractures caused by jumping into a river
to cleanse hands inclined to become mannerists,
a body that cannot be confessed.

There is the smoke of civilization
that grows up taller than we are,
and scatters first.
We meet
inside a dead history
where past ages are laughing.

Autumn Scene

In the heart of remote mountain ranges I wander shouting as I seek, turned into a wild animal destroying the whole season with its rain falling, snow falling, wind blowing. My eyes grow dim, eyelids stick, my feet are bruised. Before the year changes and I grow too old, I kindle a bonfire on top of this autumn. The wind blows. The flames spread wide. The lonely, weary souls all over the mountains burn, the mountain burns; I burn too, then once the universe is pure, at last you come into view and as I leap over the lotus blossom's night and day, we meet, caress, renounce. But with everything ultimately burned and turned to charcoal, if we stay holding hands, in about a thousand years young lovers setting fire to that charcoal will see us still burning bright and warm and feel afraid.

Telephone

Because I know you are not in
I phone you.
The ringing tone.

The ringing of the telephone now making the bookcase in your room vibrate slightly. I wait, holding the receiver to my ear for a long time, until your room is completely full of the sound of the telephone. So that when you open the door on returning home, all the telephone sounds that I have sent from this little corner will come rushing out at you, rubbing against your lips, your breast, and will watch over you all night long with the eyes of that hushed sound.

I phone again.
The ringing tone.

A Secret II

Our secret is a bed of reeds,
a reed bed lighter than the wind,
chipped, empty air with no remains,
that does not resonate, no matter how much you shake it.
So it cannot be seen,
it's merely a shadow following us,
the nonexistent trace of a shadow following us.
Why, winter is going past again.
Where has that deep winter of repose gone?
Now is shivering wordlessly at the yearly cold
but we know, believe dazzlingly, for sure.
At last, that secret's bright awakening.

Your gesture awakens me
when I again become a free man with a thirsty soul,
pushing my way through your unending reed bed.
Even though the thick flesh of broken secrets flows,
that is our foolishness, refusing to shut our eyes

As I Give You a Cloud

This cloud is sure to turn into rain.
Raindrops falling in mountain valleys
start to make watery sounds in early summer.
Those initial sounds may be small, awkward ones but,
ah, bird sipping the stream as you grow,
the blood you shed before you are fully grown
will soak into the ground and turn into a crimson wild flower,
the wild flower will rot and swoon.

But we utter formalists
will fade into falling night.
Let's be off, before night falls.
For all stationary things are death,
and love is mere astonishment.

Thus I give you a cloud,
give you the cloud of a wildflower.

A Promise

It may have been in 1962, it was autumn for sure,
sunlight filling my hands in Koyang county, Kyônggi Province,
there was a promise I made that year
to the cosmos flowers blooming in front of that government shack—
after I graduate, I'll come out somewhere in this direction;
grinding petals, I'll produce potions by the skills I've acquired,
take care of sick children, and sing.

There's a promise I made that year,
as I stood with a newly bought stethoscope round my neck,
one day when the whole world's silence was asleep.
Now all that is smashed and gone
but the same blood flows on hidden in my body;
it's autumn in this other land too and
I can still see my hands touching a petal.

from

Invisible Land of Love

(1980)

Drawing

I began to draw.
I decided to become as simple as winter.
The tree outside the window's asleep.
A snowdrift of forms
piles up in the wanderer's bones.

I began to draw a jar.
I decided to live like an empty field.
All the rest should rot
and turn into wine for a thirsty man;
for the sake of the grass of ungrown love
I began to lick a dark, long inner road.

The Secret of Adulthood

Whisper, "The End."
The bare trees scattered, unclean, across the plains
know, they know
the sound—clutching at one another from early evening,
clashing together, hurting, weeping.

If you risk your life, everything will be
fearful, beautiful.
I too long to caress the delicate skin
of a love that risks its life.

Furling the wings of adulthood—
endless though flying on and on—
I shut the window. I shut out
all the sorrows of light.

The Wind Speaks

After we have all departed this life,
should my soul brush past your face
do not for one moment think
it's just the wind that shakes the springtime branches.

I intend to plant a flowering tree today
in a scrap of shade on that spot
where I encountered you,
then once that tree has grown and blossoms,
all the torments that we have known
will turn into petals and drift away.

Turning into petals, they drift away.
It may be too remote and pointless a task
but, after all, aren't all the things we do down here
measured with so brief a yardstick?
As you sometimes pay heed to the blowing wind,
my gentle dear, never forget, no matter how weary,
the words of the wind from far, far away.

A Frog

I.

When I was a pre-med student, we used to take a frog, fix its legs to a board, cut open its belly while it was still alive, fumble with its innards and memorize: this is a kidney, this the heart, so I knew the structures of a frog's innards but what had that to do with the frog? I reckon all the frog wanted was to die quickly.

In those days, Bulgwang-dong in northern Seoul was open country and one day there I caught a frog, boiled it, picked out the bones, bleached them and stuck them together with white nail varnish; but there again, that white, beautiful, fragrant skeleton had nothing to do with the frog.

Farewell, you few flowers that suddenly strike my eye, you few flowers that in that season bled and went your ways. Goodbye to you all, our beauty and courage, still unrefined even after we admit that we have nothing at all to do with each other!

2.

I live like a frog.
Eat when hungry, sleep when night comes,
at weekends take
a hot bath.

In suitably low-lying water,
on a suitably lofty hill,
counting gray hairs
applying lotion between wrinkles,
thoughtlessly practicing adaptation to circumstances.

Rinsing my hoarse voice, rinsing my ears,
sometimes roasting barley husks
to make barley tea to drink,
practicing living between being and not, like plain water.

The riddle of turning into a frog.
The riddle of an aging frog.

The Site of the Confucian School

The site of the Confucian school—there they shot an innocent village leader, tied to a pine tree. His eyes wide open, blood was gushing from his forehead. The first time I saw someone kill another person was near the start of the War, when I was in sixth grade.

On the evening before Seoul was recaptured on September 28, fires blazing like towering hills on all sides, the site of the Confucian school—I'd gone to steal rice from a hidden stock. In the midst of gaunt ghosts fleeing, rolling and dying, shooting. Filling sacks with rice, we fled. We were just so famished.

Still there, the site of the Confucian school, when we returned after years as refugees. Still spread about with gaunt pines, a bit cold and spooky but I went there alone one snowy evening, intent on love. In those days I reckoned you could only become a good poet by loving everything in the world.

The site of the Confucian school—I went back there sometimes after I'd become a paltry poet, a paltry doctor. It was parched, naked, covered in dust, but the sight of my childhood sweat calmed my heart; now I've become a traveller in a distant land, sometimes I come across it in dreams, hear the beloved voice that used to bid me *Come, come,* and waking late at night with pillow wet, gaze once again at the site of the Confucian school.

Fishing

I'm fishing.
Too sleepy to watch the float at midday,
I suddenly wonder why fish
live day by day like that in the water?

Why do fish live?
Why does a worm live?
Why would a fish spend its whole lifetime
just swimming?

While fishing, in daylight
my body suddenly felt boiling;
I cannot go on living like this!
Flat on the earthen floor of middle age,
I cried like a fish.

Invisible Land of Love

1. Hemp from Okchô

    During a Korean history lesson in middle school, we learned about a small country called Okchô on the coast of Hamkyông Province. That night, in my dreams I was riding aimlessly along a narrow mountain path on a small pony, surrounded by people from Okchô. I heard someone say that I was on the way to the land of Koguryô, with a small roll of hemp hanging over the horse's back. I felt rather resentful at thus becoming a hemp merchant but I told myself it was much too late to refuse, as we crossed a pass thick with blooming wild chrysanthemums. At last we arrived at a large settlement in a foreign land and the gold-hued city gates creaked open. I cannot remember the reason now, but I heard someone say that henceforth I would have to live here, far away from home. My mother and father seemed not to belong to Koguryô, and seized with fear at the idea of having to live here alone, I buried my face in the bundle of hemp I was carrying and held back my tears. Even now I cannot forget the pungent smell rising from that bundle of hemp. With that hempen smell filling my nostrils like a form of salvation, I kept bidding people farewell. Unable to see anything, all the time making false steps, I suddenly found I had turned into a man from Okchô, dressed in hemp. Long ago, during a Korean history lesson, I learned about a small country called Okchô.

2. The River of the Year Kihae

—Sorrow flowing from flesh and blood,
the Blessed Ch'oe Ch'ang-hôp, martyred in Kihae year.

This place's wind grows beneath a dark river,
this place's flesh and blood are the direction the wind is driving.
The blood outside the Little West gate and at Saenamt'ô becomes a river
while desiccated souls come awake in rivers flowing from ancestors.
Invisible people believing in an invisible kingdom.

Executioner, wide-eyed executioner,
crazy executioner of 19th-century Chosôn,
shut your eyes, for your head is falling, your eyes are falling.
Long-living river, unfragrant river,
the sound of rain falling on a severed head
is the long, long-drawn-out sorrow of our land.

3. Dialogue

Dad, aren't you afraid?
No, it's dark.
Now where will you go?
I'll have to go first, then see.
It's not that we'll never see each other again?
No, we'll meet now and then.
Only in dark places like this?
No. We'll see each other in bright places too.
Dad, will you be going to your country?
In any case, that's where my fancy lies.
Didn't you enjoy being here?
Of course I enjoyed it.
Then why are you intent on going?
It's bound to be a dreary thing.
Are there dreary things even after you die?
It's all the same. Dark.
You like a country where you have no house or car?
It's still my country.
There are lots of countries. What's so special about a country?
It's because your grandfather's there.
Isn't he dead?
He's there.
Is that all?
Because I have friends there.
Could there still be friends who remember you?
Even if not, there are still friends there.
What's the good of friends who don't remember you?
Because I love them.
Surely love can flourish anywhere?
Anywhere does not feel like being alive.
Then is it in order to remember love that you write poems, Dad?
I wrote to kindle a flame because it's dark.

You mean poetry's a flame?
Because it was a lamp for me.
But didn't you find it dark all the same?
The lamp kept going out.
Can you see the country you love?
Because there's a lamp.
Still, surely it's too far off to be seen?
Because there's a lamp.

Dad, be sure to come back again. It may be the thing you've been seek-ing is not there. Still, seek all the same. So don't wander lost any more, Dad.

The snow that had fallen all night finally stopped. Now I can set out again. Since I left my homeland long ago the deeply piled snow makes this a world in which not one footstep can be discerned, but before I become a snowman and collapse, I will rise and set out on my journey.

from

How Should Living Together
Be Only for Reeds?
(1986)

Our Background

—A concert by the pianist Pollini

Two white birds flew upward
against a white background.
The birds were unseen,
all I could hear was a sound of wings.
You shook your head, No,
but I wanted to live,
even invisible, following a single path.

In this deep and difficult season
even when we do not speak
our ears hear
and even not holding hands
our palms grow moist.

Two white birds fly up again
against an empty background.
A little drop of love comes splashing down,
awake in a dark place.

The Physiology of Blood

1.

Inside our veins
mountain fires often rage.
All about us crashing noises
arouse themselves from long sleep.
Beautiful, hot blood,
blood that ever stands in our way,
blood that has lost its way expands.
That expanded blood, the mountain fires
of long feuding ancestors, burns.

2.

If red corpuscles and white corpuscles go out in mutual battle, the whole body grows dark. What clamors in us, 'Let's not fight!' are the lees of blood, the platelets. The lees of blood are tiny. The lees of blood are many. The shapes of the lees of the circulating blood are multiple. The ideas of the lees lightly floating in blood are all the same. The lees of blood heal painful and unfair wounds. Since many lees of blood die and die again, wounds heal.

The Uses of a Poet I

I want to become a poet.
What are the uses of a poet?
In Ethiopia, in Somalia,
in Central Africa,
hundreds, thousands of children, desiccated, blackened,
their skin roughened by constant starvation
die every day like so much trash.
Those children in Cambodia, Vietnam
who today play rolling skulls about
and tomorrow die in the jungle mud.
Learning to kill at ten years old,
firing machine guns at twelve.
In El Salvador, Nicaragua,
Central and South America,
all day long from sunrise to sunset
right chews at left,
left hacks at right,
head eats tail,
tail bludgeons head to death.
Every day a never-ending sound of guns,
an unceasing stream of murders.
God, what use can a poet be?

In Iran, Iraq, in Israel,
in Lebanon, the steppes of Siberia,
in every corner of the world,
God, what use can a poet be?
If we hear of others' sorrows
we weep, our hearts ache;
if people finally rise up when pain is done
we are so moved that we stamp, hiding in the bathroom.
A poet's songs of struggle may be heroic,
until those sufferings happen to me,
and though a poet's songs of consolation may feel sad,

still, God, who told us not to fall into temptation,
what use can a poet be?

Melancholy Water

Without a hot breeze blowing
a flame
is nothing more than a moving
shadow.

Melancholy of a world grown stable,
every flame complete as a painting.
Most of my sufferings
are that melancholy water.

Sometimes I
think of that day.
The trembling sound of approaching feet
bearing the waters of innocence in both hands.
I long to wash
in that full sound of water.

Water that does not tremble
is nothing more than a wet
weight.

Water Burial

—for Tong-gyu with his "Wind Burial," from abroad

From the start you studied things unseen
so a virtually invisible wind will surely be best,
whereas I studied by cutting up corpses
so I am going to have to renounce my most hidden parts.
Water, visible, endlessly visible unsubstantial water—
I shall have to be cast clearly into that water.

So let me be given water burial.
Not abroad, but just this once in Korean seas,
in the East Sea, or the Yellow Sea or the Southern Sea, anywhere,
but not too far out, somewhere close to the shore,
such was my journey throughout my whole life
but one misty evening with an old wooden boat drifting lost,
when dusk once again strikes its head against the silent sea and weeps,
like the death of a brave man who doesn't hide his shame and ignorance.

Let me be given water burial.
Shrouded in the sweaty clothes of my school days' war and poverty,
my feet bound with the senselessly heavy burden of loneliness,
somewhere in the middle of a beggar's song sung in place of a paean
cast me in without making much of a splash.

It will suddenly grow cool and silent.
After rocking gently for several days, dreaming a lengthy dream,
swarms of all those kinds of fish often seen on Korean supper tables,
hair-tails and mackerel, will eat up, eat up my flesh,
then when those plump fish, caught by fishermen, are brought to harbor
even the fishwives' stingy eyes will shine with enthusiasm.

Meanwhile I shall have become a thoughtful cloud,
or a seagull finely feathered flying above the sea,
so let me be given water burial.
My flesh once become the flesh of all those nephews, nieces,
as I play, running down this alley and that,
the time of thick fog I wandered in so long in life will end
and at last I shall open blazing eyes.

Singing for a Dead Tree

A dead tree
stays standing even after death.
Several years of fallen leaves, eager to turn into earth
knock at the ground's heavy doors
amidst the moans of insects
that cannot sleep even at night.

Perhaps it's weary?
The thick fog that embraces shattered stones
and various landscapes weary from fleeing
lean weeping against the dead tree.

Winter snows will soon come.
Days spent with windows wide open will pass
and with eyes full of fear, of many doubts,
you will cold-bloodedly chop up the tree that died standing
to gain warmth in winter's chill.

The dead tree is burning.
As it burns, the dead tree speaks,
as it sets out at last, hand in hand with the wind,
the dead tree's soul, the dead tree's soul . . .

South-American-style Winter

I.

Sailors in the navy stirred up a revolution at sea.
Wearing black uniforms, carrying weapons,
all keeping step with the towering waves,
they stirred up a revolution.
The moon floating above the sea weeps.
The revolution that can never land
is swept away by the whole world's wind and waves.
The tomb of all those missing at sea
rises when night falls, radiant above the waves,

2.

The Andes grow taller in winter.
Piled dazzling with millions upon millions of snowflakes,
mountain paths more clearly visible the darker it gets,
the Andes serve as the angels' playground,
friends of Saint Exupéry gone missing
come dropping all winter long like flowers on this foreign land
and descend the hills like songs of my longed-for home.

Between the Andes and the nation and sea,
robed in the longest cloak in the world,
wearing the longest decoration in the world,
pierced by any number of bullets,
smiling, shaking hands, making promises
the dark soul of the high-waved sea
strikes against the long, wintery peaks and breaks.
When an earthquake with unending echoes
covers the nation, gone utterly missing,
you, cutting off both your frostbitten hands
without shedding a tear, you.

A Poem in a Foreign Tongue

One winter evening in a freezing hall
the snowstorm outside roared even louder
as suddenly Czeslaw Milosz, the Nobel laureate,
began to recite one of his poems in Polish.
The trees standing out there in the snow
became more clearly visible.
One winter's evening in the Midwest, a nondescript town,
the audience taken aback, darkness all around,
and Milosz's poem, with not a word we could understand,
filled the stage, spilled over and turned into a blizzard.
The dreams of nomads, often reduced to gnawing dry crusts
amidst the ashen skies, rivers, forests
of old eastern Europe, beetle-browed,
one winter night's unquenchable thirst.

Night Song IV

How should living together be only for reeds?
How should a life spent rubbing shoulders
on windswept hills, on dark river banks, only be for reeds?
Though every night wolves howl in barren mountain gorges,
rising again together after falling flat, brushing off the dust—
how should that only be for our nation's reeds?

From far away, you look pale and blue;
seen close up you look sad.
A few clouds rising from hills toward higher hills,
clouds that by night turn into pure moisture and make pillows wet,
wander, grow timid, turn into rain,
falling on you in the far-off reed-bed where I once lived,
while not even deep night's darkness can hide my foolishness.

Prayer

Lord God,
may I weep for no reason.
Then may I see you
in those tears,
meet others
in those tears

and once I am dead
may I live by their tears.

from

The Color of That Country's Sky

(1991)

Drawing IV

1.

I am drawing a single tree. A tree that decided
to live alone, lonesome though it might be
Last summer was noisy. A tree that now
stands listening to the unprofitable sound of rain
with a few empty birds' nests hanging like decorations.
In the dark, birds from all sides still fly away
like groundless rumors, a temptation.
A temptation for my whole life weeping ceaselessly.

2.

Nowadays, I take great interest
in a tree of about my own age.
Even when large branches are cut off
it cannot feel it for long and
it is only after a mountain breeze, briefly blinking,
has passed and gone that it feels inwardly chilled.
After all the leaves of destiny have flown away
what can it be pointing toward
with the grayish tip of its lofty branches, calling, calling.

Wife Asleep

Waking suddenly in the middle of the night,
I hear my wife of the past twenty years lying beside me
talking in her sleep with little weeping sounds.
Moans too can be heard from time to time.
The world can be better seen with the lights out.

Perhaps the sound our lives make, heard from far off,
is all a moaning sound.
In any case, we can only be each one alone,
and coming to know that is of no importance
but wife, learning to weep lightly in your sleep—
in the end, that's your deepest destiny.

Once Dried Anchovies Have Flavored the Soup is that the End?

(One by one my wife picked the anchovies out of the tasty
boiling soup and threw them away. You have to take them out
of the soup once it's done. They're unsightly and have no taste left.)
Once dried anchovies have flavored the soup is that the end?

And in those difficult years, fiercely boiling times,
dried anchovies hurled themselves in, here and there.
(The fish must have screamed: It's hot;
I'm panting; It hurts; It's dark. Caught in shoals,
dried raw, their bodies utterly emaciated,
hear the screams of the writhing fish.)

Now, as we eat the refreshing, tasty soup,
we should remember the dried anchovies, swept away.
(We should remember the shoals of young anchovies, silver scaled,
swimming fresh in the gentle billows of the Southern Sea.
At last that long winter is nearly over.)

Reeds' Blood

The reason why I like reeds
is because they live as if they were dead.
It must be the way they sway as if alive
when in fact they are dead.

Alive and dead mingled, nicely matched,
dead reeds sing in harmony with live ones
live reeds dance holding dead ones in their arms.

Spending whole lifetimes quite distracted,
readily accepting separation from their bodies,
they laugh as they wave goodbye.

Since they care for each other, they waste no words,
no touch of a hand, no shoulder embraced.
I want to embrace you, white reed blossoms drifting!
You never let anyone see the blood you shed every day.

Late Autumn Sea

Why, our peace has drawn lightly near
and is blending with its brothers' flow.
Look! Curdling, rolling, they're becoming one.
Turn into a current, then vanish from sight.
I am comforting you, whose depths are invisible.

Like a white wave from days gone by,
if our bodies meet in such an encounter
you, unable to avoid it, will become a flower.
That flower will become a blossoming gesture.

As the sea, already abruptly darkening,
narrows in all directions, my eyes quickly grow clear
and since there is no longer any sound of waves,
my ears grow much clearer too.

In this year's last autumn moment with shoulders hunched,
I'll leave you alone close to an evening where no one is near,
two shameful hands from trembling Purgatory.
Just stay there alone. Out in the midst of the empty sea
your hazy face is moving away.

The Hill Inside the Hill

Inside each hill is another hill.
Inside the hill we can see with our eyes
a hill is living, hidden.
If we climb the hill, we can hear
very vividly what the hill is saying.
Inside the skin of the rough hill
the fragrance of a deep, soft hill.

If there is no water inside the water,
we'll not be visible in the water.
Even if you went out alone to the sea
you'd not be able to hear words coming from far away.

So, inevitably, there's an I inside me,
a life smaller than I living hidden inside me,
a soul of words that can be heard when I'm quiet.

A Rainy Day

When clouds meet,
loud thunder emerges.
I long for a meeting like that with you,
where I would cry out, unthinkingly.

When clouds suddenly meet,
bright lightning flashes all at once.
I long to rediscover, meeting you,
the bright flame I have lost.

I cannot sing along together with
the highs and lows of the song the rain sings
but you teach me brightly that
raindrops can make each other wet only if they meet.

Drifting Song

On the frantic road to work
I should select a roadside tree
then one day, as night is falling, build
a birds' nest high in that tree.
At times when life is dizzying and harsh
I should turn into a light bird, and go take some rest.
To avoid frightening the neighboring birds,
I would have to avoid all sudden gestures, hush my voice,
and if some drifting soul shows interest
that cold heart too should go take some rest.

Throwing open the doors of the nest, what shall I do?
Shall I wash away the wind smeared over my face?
If they attach no conditions, they are all so light.
Though our intolerable tales, too, meeting easily,
make their way within you and ask to sleep,
they are laughing now, perhaps no longer hurting.

Remembering Vincent

I The Winter Bride

My brother, much missed,
winter is truly
hard to live through.

The windows of my soul
are all iced over.
The landscape I long for is quite invisible
while the dark, damp streets
are all motionless.

Maybe devoted love
is made perfect
when people are cold.

Vincent van Gogh's decision
to set up house with a beggar woman
about to give birth as his newly-wed bride
never leaves us.
Behind it snow falls
and a few anonymous flakes
incapable of thinking straight
end up hugging one another.

2 The Color of the Wind

Do you see the wind in my paintings?
If you take away the wind, I'm just a dead flower.

I'm going to build a house in a flower.
Once the flower has ripened, just as it's waking up,
the departing wind waves a hand.
Theo! Time is a revelation.

I must announce it before winter comes.
My profession, breathlessly lived and unsuitable
will appear one day as fruits at the tip of branches.
As you nibble their flesh, brother, I wonder
if you'll be able to taste all the bitters and sweets of this world's winds.

So I'm rich.
I have spent my whole life turning into wind.
There's no need for you to send any more money.
I see how my life turns into many winds
and spreads across the world as a shining joy.

3 Chinese Vincent

Who killed Vincent?

(Vincent, a young Chinaman in his twenties, died after having his head beaten to pulp by a white man's cudgel, who set about him without warning in a bar in Detroit, city of cars. It seems that after he'd been sacked from the car factory, he was often heard to proclaim when he was drunk that all the Orientals ought to be killed. Claiming that it was imported Asian cars produced with cheap labor that had cost him his job, he struck him in a drunken fury as if he was demolishing a Japanese car.)

Who killed Vincent?

(In court, the white judge handed down a light sentence of two years in jail, commenting that he was being specially lenient, since he had acted when drunk, then a little later allowed the white murderer to leave jail, a free man.)

Who killed Vincent?

(We demonstrated. "We demand a fair trial! No discrimination against Asians!" we shouted in the city center, everyone passing by with averted eyes, snow falling, we shouted, shook our fists at the invisible winter sky, and my face as I turn homeward, weary, why, it's still burning hot.)

Who killed old Vincent?

(Theo, you think I'm laughable, don't you, coming empty-handed to this foreign land then pointlessly pretending to be victimized? You want to ask who told me to live in the U.S., don't you? I agree, you're quite right. But you'd better reflect too. People are still hitting and killing people, for having a different political color, something slighter than skin color. And thrusting their heads into tubs of water, too.)

Who killed our old Vincent?

4. Freedom Remembered

Theo, I longed to become someone completely free.
That's why I left home when still young.
I knew that someone free was bound to be lonely.
When I called freedom's name I was alone.

Theo, freedom was my sole possibility.
Someone free does not interfere or constrain.
I never wanted to wear handcuffs again.
I never called anyone's name.

I'll make no excuses.
Nowadays ten suns can be seen at once.
A few of the suns can be heard speaking as they shake.
Ceaselessly, the wide open plains glimpsed through the bars
are all fluttering about, day and night.
A frenzied dance enflames my body.
I am eager to show you.
The sky glides down to the plains
where trees and plants and clouds embrace and weep.

Theo, listen carefully to what I am saying.
I may never be able to go back home.
The collapsing buildings of this asylum have caught hold of me
and won't let go.
I really wanted to live with you back home once more.

I miss the people back home peeling potatoes.
But perfect Dutch slogans are foreign to me,
the whirling beams of justice, resolute battle-cries are not things
I would exchange for the feverish dances I have developed alone.

Theo, the path I have to take is still long-drawn-out and hard.
I often long to mingle with those shouting thickets.
I long at last to greet my quiet evening in those thickets.
I long to rest, dreaming endless dreams.
The strong odor of freedom is summoning me again.

Splendor of Water IV

When I think of how, once I am dead, I shall turn into water, it sometimes makes me melancholy. When I flow down, mingled with the water of a mountain ditch, I don't suppose anyone will recognize my voice as they listen to that little babbling sound. Even when I have mingled with that stream and turned into water, I won't be clean at first. As I flow and flow, gradually the sins committed in my life will be washed away, the lingering grudges linked to my life will be washed away too, the lonely nights, the residual sorrows, will all be washed away one after another, until at last I have turned into pure water, all desires cast off. If I am able to turn into really pure water, then I will call you. View yourself reflected in that water. Listen attentively to my voice. Laughing, having rid myself of all extravagant gestures, I shall confess that I wanted to live long years with you. Then for the first time at last you will possess me wholly, body and mind. Do you know what it means to say that someone possesses someone else entirely? Then scoop up that water, wash your hands, moisten your throat. That will remove the thirst of your weary times. And inside you I shall become you. Finally I shall realize that having turned into water after my death was not at all a reason for melancholy.

Summer Letter

Reckless summer!
Here and there flowers
have got themselves into pregnancies
they will be unable to take responsibility for,
while grass too, trees too, I too
when summer comes, climb onto roofs
like thieves.

How many skies
were there up there on the roof?
Vague oaths went secretly
flowing away in all directions,
turning into quick-winged birds,
made every direction unsteady.
Yes, really unsteady.
All those promises made us weep
beautifully, like fragrance.

Destitute summer.
The sky we trusted
was gray as a cloud
while a trumpet played high and low
and danced.
And we slept.
The rain falling in our dreams
drenched the summer
and until the moisture remaining on our skin
had turned its face away coldly,
we went riding on the wind.

Blue birds and wrens
refused to show us
the way back home.
From that summer on
we began to grow old.

from

Eyes of Dew

(1997)

Visitor

On opening the heavy door, I found
winter had arrived.
Welcome snowflakes were falling from every side
and the winds between the snowflakes
were embracing the bare trees like life.
Our destined meeting came about like that.

The snow-covered white trees were
drawing closer to one another.
Crowded, tenacious roads had been erased
and every sea was returning shoreward,
while the sky that had so lightly risen
slowly sank down to become the ground.

But visitors always leave.
With my two empty hands I receive
the peace you transmit.

Eyes of Dew

I went up into the mountains; there autumn was layered deep
and I stood there holding an empty bowl.
After I had survived a whole night's bitter cold,
I saw clear dew had gathered in the bowl.
But there was so little dew
it could not quench my thirst.
If I collect it for a second night, will there be more?
If I spend days gazing into the eyes of the dew,
will I be able to save one pure, chill poem?
Quench a causeless thirst?

The next day before dawn, instead of dew
one dead leaf fell onto my shoulder
and by dint of shouting: Vanity, all vanity,
it brought me to my knees, shoulders burdened.
Only when morning came did the dew open clear eyes
and give value to the night's dead leaf.
—Live with both eyes open.
Look ahead, look behind, look up.
You can see everything. You come and you go,
until you have gathered all yourselves, and after that too,
live with both eyes open, like wind or sea.
Living like wind or hill or sea, I
saw the two eyes of the dew. And after that too
in the front of the wind or the back of the sea
I saw the two open eyes of the dew.

Splendor of Water XI

Shattering, water
becomes many drops.
Shattering, water
becomes many offspring.
Water-drops are tiny
but fill many places to overflowing
then their color spreads everywhere.
The offspring are brighter,
more beautiful than their parents.
If water's father does not shatter
nothing bright can come to birth.
Once water-drops gather in some low place
they become father. That's why
our father is always lowest.
In that deep interior where water's body moves
the words of the water's aging splendor
draw near refreshingly one by one.

The Island

Yôûido was flooded that summer.
In days before apartments and the National Assembly were built
I underwent interrogation there in Basement Room 3.
I have no idea if the Military Personnel Law still exists but
the guy writing down my deposition had a harsh voice and big hands.

All that summer I kept thinking of an island.
As we were dragged in fetters along the streets of Yôngdûngp'o
where the asphalt was melting, bound in a line like so many dried fish,
I was thinking of one carefree little island.
I longed to turn into a weed and live on a sunny hillside there.

My iron-barred cell with its musty stench was small and stuffy.
With meals of a lump of barley-mixed rice, my stomach ached
Once the noisy bedtime roll-call by an armed soldier was done,
late at night I dreamed of escaping from my cell.
An island without noisy birdsong and with no flowers in bloom.

The waves of the sea were gentle green or silver.
My military doctor's badge of rank torn off, my beard growing scraggily,
belt and shoelaces removed 'to prevent attempted suicide,'
as I dragged about my youthful body and feet heavy with insults
I longed to lie down by that sea, shut my eyes and let time pass.

When friends who came to visit left in tears, horrified at my appearance,
when they urged me: Comrade, don't let them win, be a hero,
I banished all mention of escape and exile far from my lips,
resolved that I would definitely go to that island.
An island without winning or losing, an island devoid of heroes.

Once I was freed, thoughtless, the first thing I did was set out.
But when I realized that the place I had reached was not my island
my father had already died and I had a family to support.
That wonderful island I saw every day all that summer!
I still often dream about it. That quiet island's smile,
that cozy island, floating somewhere, its tears.

In a Cemetery

I.

My younger brother, dead, buried in a foreign cemetery
where the grass has still not grown properly after a year.
I lean against the headstone with the name carved in Korean.
With you below the ground, and above it a few scraps of lowering sky,
where are we in this easy-going life-span?

2.

Even after you were gone, every day the sun would rise and night would
fall. Although you met your end down a road you took by mistake,
thanks! You lived all through these past decades at my side as a kind lit-
tle brother, though sometimes you must have been hurt by kicks from
my cocksure heart. Until that day when we meet again and weep leaping
for joy, setbacks melting, resentments melting, heavens melting—keep
well! Keep well in deep deep breathing.

3.

All the air near a cemetery is always plunged deep in thought.
The air near a cemetery is always gazing into the distance.
A quiet, full smell is spreading in all directions.
I murmur to the ground, still brown though a year has passed,
that it still hurts too much inside me.
A bird that had been singing afar abruptly closes its beak.
The air in the cemetery loses its strength and sinks under the ground.

Autumn Mountain

When in ancient times I wove my way
through the world in the shape of the wind,
making no distinction between high and low,
striking, hugging, rolling about,
the hill often averted her eyes from me.

Now I can hear sounds I used not to hear;
the evening of my life comes amidst the low hills
where the sounds live together.
No words from my kind companion of blue clouds;
only that empty landscape fills me fully.

Oh, you light gathered on the autumn hills,
brilliant color of the dead leaves on the trees
color of souls!
Even my wind, that had lived in hiding
turns into colorful dancing and comes back again.

Alone

In Asia Minor, Turkey, making a trip to the New Testament city of Ephesus, my feet were feeling the early church's preaching, persecution, earthquakes, having heard Saint Paul's heated voice echo in the completely ruined ancient city, passed the markets where once there were many jewellers, peeped at the abandoned street where he had once hidden in a prostitute's house, after criss-crossing the empty city for half a day, as I emerged through the city's back gate, the sadly majestic images from two thousand years ago abruptly vanished and a poor village market place, cheap stalls in a line, was offering dust-covered souvenirs for sale. Fleeing from the clamor of a rushing hoard of touts, confused for a moment I saw myself drawing close, a young peddler, just as I had been a newspaper boy as a wartime refugee, .:

"You Korean? You Japanese?"
"Am I Korean? You bet I'm Korean."
"Come. My mother Korean! My mother Korean!"
Following in bewilderment, inside the tent composing the stall
a poorly-dressed Korean woman in her late thirties bowed her head.
"You Korean?" — Yes.
"Glad to meet you." — Yes.
"How long here?" — About fifteen years . . .
"Any other Koreans around here?" — Alone . . .
"All alone?" (in this dust!) — Yes . . .
"I've been living abroad for over twenty years too."
"Ah, yes. Twenty years . . ."
In weary eyes, piled up, another land's dust.

Glimpsing her Turkish husband prowling around nearby, I buy a cheap tee-shirt with a bunch of flags decorating the front, and from the boy, who is gazing up at me in triumph, I buy some horn flutes then, flustered, prepare to leave. "Good luck." "Yes, good-bye." Even in Turkey, we take our leave in Korean style. I get into our bus, carrying my purchases. Among all the white faces, one yellow spot. The barefooted boy, standing at the roadside, is waving a hand and smiling. I look out again. The

boy has vanished and raindrops are beginning to strike against the win-
dow. All alone, I said? Idiot! Alone . . . Suddenly, walking alone toward
the endless reedbeds surrounding Ephesus, moistened by the light rain,
my beloved, lonesome God.

Mountainward II

Why, even the trees weep early in the morning.
They are weeping the dew that gathers all night
before I can lay even a hand on their thin shoulders.
Who will ever wipe clean away every trace of loneliness?
Still gently trembling bygone days!
Taking advantage of a brief rest, I look round.
On this trip to the mountains, begun without asking directions,
whom will I blame if the summit cannot be seen?
I adjust my backpack, prepare to set off again
along a path soaked as far as sight can see.

This World's Long River

I.

Evening falls early, and as the hill's shadow comes strolling out
and begins to cover the broad twilight river
the ripples on the ancient river shrink conspicuously
while the river's name and nationality grow increasingly vague.

If I station myself at the edge of the river of uncertain nationality
and, calling together my present state that often goes astray,
spend the night listening to the lapping water,
your bodies and mine, with their uncertain nationalities,
will soak in all the water in this river of unknown depth and
ah, since people are linked in this way by water
we should realize we all share the same hometown.

Finally the heavy night yields and dawn filters through.
The river's multitude of eyes, all sparkling,
the river's waters mingle, jostling bodies.
Ah, by the river's glow, that I saw somewhere in my youth,
as we advance in a similar direction, as if we are one,
we realize: together we shall not succumb, though we go astray.

2.

For several days I stayed alone on the banks of a long river. No radio, no television, no literature or art or music. Everything I had was alive. Music was alive between water and rocks, on the lips of dew on grass meeting other dewdrops art was alive. Poems were living on the antennae of insects feeling their way along the ground, novels lived in those insects' long, leisurely itineraries.

Everything was moving. Water, leaves, clouds, birds and small animals, all were moving ceaselessly; raindrops, the chirping of insects by night, sunlight by day, moonlight by night, the colors of the river, and all their shadows were moving. That moving world drove me away from my surroundings, made me move. I abandoned myself completely and began to breathe in imitation of the breathing of the luxuriant foliage.

At last I was enabled to acknowledge my very flesh as something alive and breathing. My breathing body, once it had escaped the complicated commands of my anxious head, began to grow calm. My shoulders grew light, my eyes clear, able to see fruit hiding in spiders' webs, and love songs vibrating insects' wings. At last I realized that everything in the world had become one and was moving.

Everything in the world was one. There could be no other way. So I determined to abandon distinctions between things big and small, between things visible and invisible, to abandon distinctions between things living and dead. Those were difficult decisions for me. A few days later, as I left the river bank, where there was no trace of human life, I took my leave; at once the river approached without a word and placed a few long rivers in my heart. So I became a river.

A Reed

Why do all those mindless reeds that live along windy roadsides
or on distant river banks all grow to exactly the same height?
If just a few grew taller, they would be snapped off by the wind
and if just a few grew smaller they would wither for lack of sunlight,
so perhaps they know how easy it is to catch one's death
and therefore the reeds all grow as one, putting their heads together.

The tall reed often bows its head humbly,
and all dance to the same beat, none rich or poor.
There's a bad rumor going around, tucked into their belts;
giggling at the same height with friends in all directions,
the reeds make grabs at each other, and sleep together too,
ah, the reedbed! Such a festive gathering!
I want to grow old with you.

Back in Seoul, that war had reduced to ruins, sheltered from the wind by a flapping tent that served as a makeshift school room, I found myself memorizing the difference between an Ionian building and a Corinthian building. That winter was particularly cold and dry, so at some point I began to hunch my shoulders from midday on and dream fantastic day-dreams in which I had built a classy Ionian style house, sat in a leather armchair heated by a steam-fed system, and resolved to break the wrists of the dreadful cold. (Yes, an Ionian style house!)

I wonder if our childhood hunger also had its origins in Ionia. Every few days, with the money father got for writing, I would buy two small measures of rice and as I carried that light bagful on my shoulder through the mud of the marketplace, I was gazing at the Greek coast, the emerald hues of the Ionian Sea. The Ionian Sea clamorous with celebra-tions, tasty bread and grapes, the Ionian Sea idly tossing dazzling white ships, and I many times resolved I would not become a hungry writer.

The Ionian Sea I finally managed to reach when I had already passed my half-century had gentle waves just like those in my childhood dreams and the water was clear, but it was a sick sea, an empty nest from which the plentiful shoals of fish had all vanished. The Ionian style columns were dirty, too; they'd become gap-toothed old men. Well, of course, a long time had passed. Ionia, old and feeble, my foolish resolve has van-ished away, and I am still roaming the world, hungry.

Hoping for What Can Be Seen is No Hope

Having smacked my lips for a number of years over a friend's letter
    describing
walking along the river embankment on the way to visit Hahoi Village,
having a drink in Dasan's cottage in Kangjin, savoring the lovely river
    with it,
but since hoping for what can be seen is no hope,
so too the little feet of a saint rising from a stony bed and setting forth
erased from his eyes the scented wild flowers of Italy,
erasing too the secrets of the wide-stretching highlands with their
    sunrise and sunset.
Since hoping for what can be seen is no hope,
after long sharing the fate of birds seemingly linked to me by blood,
    and life here below,
after tidying away little hills that have abandoned their first name
    and last name too,
I open all my body's doors frantically, like one possessed.
Above my head a number of skies have gathered and are holding hands.
Since hoping for what can be seen is no hope,
advancing amidst the breathing of an unseen land, words of a voice
    unheard,
a comforting moment that has painfully made its way here from afar.

Note: "Since hoping for what can be seen is no hope." —Romans 8:24.

from

In the Birds' Dreams Trees are Fragrant

(2002)

Wave

Silly wave.
You cry out as you strike your breast day and night
against the house-sized rocks littering this shore,
but all you get is a white blood of foam.
It would take three hundred years at least
to turn them into a sandy beach
where you can roll about with pleasant tickling,

By that time, who will remember you?
Will you dance, curving your back?
Silly wave. Are you determined to ignore the passage of time
and just go on dreaming of thirsty storms?
The wave's hand, ever restless from far away seas,
writes a long letter, deletes it, writes it again.

Revelation in Wildflowers

I.

At the end of one whole year the Apostle John
emerges from a deep rocky cave
on Patmos, a stony islet in the Aegean Straits,
the sunlight warm as every year.

So old he cannot see too well,
he drinks a draft of rainwater set ready
then waves a hand as if to say: Love one another.
Jesus died a long while back, so
what do those flying white locks mean
as he slowly walks down the stony path?

2.

The letters John sent to the seven churches have arrived,
launched out in wooden ships across the wind and waves.
The shadow of words that long flowed down watery paths,
shredded by penalties, sequence and assumptions,
until the sincerity of love and pain are largely invisible.
The high waves' horizon too is nearly invisible.

3.

In John's cave, where he is said to have written the Book of Revelation,
a young Orthodox priest sat dozing before a stone table
on which stood one glass of water.
His clean white face on which a tall black hat was pressed down
frankly reflected the shadow cast by a complex dream.
As I emerged from the cave after climbing dozens of stone steps
the breeze residing on the island washed my face,
the wild flowers gathered in vestiges came crowding round
and whispered in muffled voices: *Love one another.*
Unsure whose voice it was on account of the waves,
the design of those words made my legs shake,
for only the intense, burning flowers were waving.

Gregorian Chant II

Ask those flying leaves over there,
ask that wind standing there in the air—
there was no one in sight on the evening shore.
Just a few seagulls screaming, scavenging, hiding,
clouds deep in thought changing the color of their flesh,
the bachelor sea blushing embarrassed.

Once on the shore I hear Gregorian chant.
Tearful confessions of an organ fill my ears.
A salt sea of Amens brings healing to wounds.
The rising tide was caressing the beach's flesh.
I turned into a little wave and approached you.
Time stopped, the evening sun gently settled down.
The tight-lipped shore began to dream peaceful dreams.
I resolved not to resent my traveller's fate.

Gregorian Chant III

The harmonious prayers of a host of celibates
once heard in the old dark monasteries of the middle ages
open high vaults and make the heavens.
In the heavens a few light flowers bloom.
Beautiful things have always been remote and featureless.
Guiding premonitions of previous lives, I start a long journey.
Escaping from the crowded, noisy city center,
I take a field path along empty riversides in dazzling sunlight.
Poplars dance, insects laugh quietly,
a warm, miraculous day filling the entire world
as I see the tears of the earth on its glowing face.

Ideas about Autumn

Ah, just look at that amazing
face of God.
Hundreds of millions of trembling points, a pointillist painting.
Those foolish-minded leaves, setting off on long journeys
saying that being alive is to dream,
dying is to awaken from dreams —

Just look at that face of God, so busy
changing colors that he gets no sleep at night.
Two straight lines leave,
not able to form a square
There is no shared destiny that knows no parting.
Leaves summon their last breath for freedom's sake
as they set off in search
of a lonely winter soldier.

The Sea's House

1.

The sea's entire being can be seen even at night.
After returning home from long wandering,
something once heard, a slender timid phrase:
the sand along the shore growing softer still and warmer
journeys on through the invisible dark air.
Ancient hills are levelled
hands guilty of sin are pardoned.

2.

Late morning, plunged deep in thought,
I long to embrace the sea's bare body
as she lies half veiling her nakedness.
A butterfly bigger than a sailing ship
settles on a petal vaster than the sea
lightly like Dufy's painting "Anemone."
The sea's house ripples under the butterfly's weight,
a few fishy smells drift from the sea
and bequeath a toy-like cloud to the sky.

3.

Today the horizon is thicker
than on ordinary days.
It looks as though it must be raining
in the sea's back yard.
Why do the waves, once so quiet,
only flinch and embrace as they reach the shore?
The waves' slight excuse—
the sea has such a good memory.
In an unfamiliar landscape
your familiar features come into view.

With Fear and Trembling

Climbing a low hill alone on a spring evening
and gazing up at the widespread sky
is to see with fear and trembling
the stars' scalding tears. On such an evening
stripping off the tattered clothes of my daily life
full of good sense, hypocrisy and embellishment
is to see with fear and trembling
the star's delicate smiles.

The earth has already fastened the dark bolts
so several worlds can be more lightly seen while
you, who I thought still far away,
the body of silence, harkening to the songs of the stars,
blink your eyes as you slowly dance,
barefoot, with fear and trembling.

Note: 'With fear and trembling': Philippians 2:12

Sesame Flowers

Sesame seeds, that lived separate lives as they slept buried in the ground, produce fragrant sesame leaves, bloom with the lovely little white sesame flowers that will one day blossom as a milky mist amidst a host of sesame leaves, and you, soil, produce moist sesame seeds before ever all the sesame flowers have been seen. What bargain have you made with the sesame seeds that you provide them with such solid, abundant bodies?

Likewise, how do all the flower-seeds I cannot see clearly with my weakening eyesight produce the fragile, delicate skin of the red and purple flowers I can see so clearly in this back garden? Where are the earth's dye factories, needlework factories, perfume factories, that enable this little flower to blossom and laugh here, its white dress girt thinly about with a pink belt?

Is it because my common sense is growing more and more vague with age that the things people incline to think normal seem to me increasingly abnormal? At least tell me, land of mystery rising on my ever vaguer common sense, if we are ever able to draw close to you, will we recognize your prudent skill? Or at least will we be able to watch and enjoy every day your charming magic as earth becomes flowers, earth becomes sesame seed?

Eye-openings of knowledge like sesame seeds, as my growing curiosity gradually finds answers; today once again I sit beside a sesame flower and wait for a flickering word, and on that day when my flesh becomes a sesame flower will you be able to recognize that my words and writing have at least been able to emit fragrance? Will you be able to recognize that the days when I wandered in search of the song I wished to sing have turned into fresh life at last?

Echo

Have you ever heard
a little lake singing?
Letting your weary mind go on sleeping,
listening like the grass in a forest at dawn,
hiding yourself in thick mist,
have you ever heard a river singing?
Rather like the sound of a long flute,
perhaps a cello, maybe an accordion;
at that bright, thin sound arriving from afar
a dawn mist slowly rises
and trembles on the water's surface—wake up now.
Ah, the rising mist dances.
In human shape, dancing,
the mist laughs as it clears the mist away.
The whole morning rises all together.
The dazzling river's echo
embraces us.

Wounds

I.

Suddenly I've
reached the age of an old man
when loveable things
just look loveable
and laughable things
simply look laughable.

The person I was in my youthful days!
Youth wretchedly contemplating
the lonely old orphan I am now!
Everything happening in the world
always settled heavily in my heart.
Emotion's pulse was easily set racing
and could nowhere easily find a place
where I might take a long rest.

2.

Yes, indeed, the person I was in my youthful days!
One single tear of God,
unable to flee, blocked for a whole lifetime,
and that lake lying far away
is likewise pitifully growing ever older.
I have several times hurled into the lake
time's long oppressing insomnia.
The lake, assuming that insomnia,
churning its whole being to the top of its head,
opens its eyes briefly, rocks to and fro.
Its tenderest flesh once washed in the wind
the lake's skin cracks open here and there,
and even its thin legs tremble.

3.

Where was I? I have suddenly
reached the age of an old man where
lake and wind and legs as well
are all remembered as nothing but a vague odor,
the illusion of an occasional clamor sometimes ringing
in my ears in places where there's no one around—
the clamor of old age with its wounds
that no one can forbid us.

Festival Flowers

If ever I were to penetrate inside a flower,
it would be warm.
Stamens and pistils live there
taking the wind or a passing gesture for pretext
secretly inclining.

Even withering flowers with heads bowed down
are warm.
Whether pregnant or not,
lying uncovered with a hint of a swoon
in a tender, soft posture,
a deeply sleeping flower.

My journey as I head toward you, too,
will be warm.
The eyes and ears of a sleeping flower
wrapped round with unfulfilled dreams,
ah, separation, token of festival!
Sad pollen will fall like confetti
and drench us both.

Some Other Sea

I will set off in search of some other sea.
The pines standing in rows along the shore,
blinded by the sea's salty air,
inquire if the sea is still alive.
A sea-wall has been laid, you have gone,
the sound of waves restless with fever has gone,
and in nights when old age makes me often wake
I inquire if the sea is still alive.

I will go in search of some other sea.
That first waterway I shyly embarked on in youth
has darkly vanished like a mirage
and all lies wrapped in a thick sea mist.
Naked stillness is warm.
The pines painfully open their arms,
bow low and whisper—the sea is alive.

Winter Tomb

As I stand before my brother's desolate tomb,
his lifetime looks so cold and fragile
that even on a snowy day my heart feels like breaking.

Living and dying are like falling snow
so although we join to affirm we are going somewhere,
that hard calculation all drops into death's void
and in today's heavy snowfall there is no one in sight.

I open my hands to receive the snow, hoping for news,
but in a flash that news turns into a tear
and a silence ripening in the ear soaks into the surrounding labyrinth.

My eyes scan in vain the freezing ash-gray sky,
snow falls, drifts cover even the gravestone.
My moving sorrow encounters his sorrow that cannot move
and look, they comfort each other by their own pure weight.

So it is. We cannot possibly part company.
Your breath is the pure cold air around this tomb
and as the sky drops lower, we hold hands.
Suddenly it stops snowing, the wind drops, and we . . .

Like a Pumpkin

Have I built my house here and put out my vines to spend my whole life like this? Intent on developing leaves and blossoming, the pumpkin found itself unable to take a holiday, and once a few baby pumkins appeared, it started to show weary wrinkles. Its leaves spread out chlorophyll all day long, received sunshine, manufactured organic nutritives, the roots pumped up water until their shoulders bent, procured inorganic substances and fed the baby pumpkins. All for the sake of my babes, to feed my seeds inside them, so that I can be reborn in them, surely?

The larger the pumpkins grew, the more food and money and devotion they required. Intent on feeding its children well and raising them far better than any others, the roots lost their strength and lay useless in the ground, the leaves too after slaving away till their backs were bent grew senile, began to rave as autumn came, then roots and stalks and leaves as they withered and died gazed at their beautifully swelling offspring, smiled pumpkin smiles and expired. I'll be reborn in them, those pumpkins are my life in another form, my glory in the next world, surely?

I may resolve that when I raise my children, it will not be for a pumpkin-like existence, but it's an illusion, an undeniable illusion. Though the pumpkin seeds from the dead leaves and roots may become huge pumpkins the following year, who will be able to identify those pumpkins as being descended from them? No matter whether yellow or reddish, insipid or sweet, small or big in size, what difference does it make whether it's called Mr. Kim or Mr. Lee or Mr. Park, whether it's from this or that region, this or that clan? Ah, my life's course, rushing out, then tottering back not many days later feeling all forlorn, just like a pumpkin.

The children you raise with such effort as a pumpkin are pumpkins, the children other people raise are pumpkins too. Your friends and relatives too, and the people you brushed past briefly yesterday, are all pumpkins. Even an only son, a pumpkin seed of a leading family, can never produce anything more than another pumpkin. This seed may be eaten up and disappear for no reason while another one's seed produces pumpkins for decades, yet, until we realize as pumpkin-like days pass in pumpkin-like ways that others' pumpkins and my pumpkins are all pumpkins alike, until we admit the pumpkin-like truth that pumpkin is pumpkin right to the core . . .

Kaeshim-sa: Open-heart Temple

Walking round a cloud-close valley
I find a temple courtyard, not one monk in sight;
a small statue of Buddha, opening its heart,
bids me come inside if I'm feeling cold.

The largest, broadest colors in the world,
divided between sunlight and shade, embrace the temple—
hunchbacked pillars bearing up heavy roofs,
twisted, tattered old wooden pillars
tell me: always keep your body firm.

Around the temple, tree roots emerge, split the ground,
stretch out along hill-paths, breath deeply
while bamboos' bare hands, frozen pale green,
wave: learn at least a scrap of widespread compassion.

The Path

Was that lofty, magnificent lighthouse just an illusion?
The port I long to visit lies soaked in icy rain
and although I still can't believe it,
someone said there's a path across the boundless ocean.
You, growing old together with me,
can you hear?

The sea breeze was soft as hidden flesh and
when chill wavelets met, exchanged their greetings,
the sea-mist-shrouded house turned down its lights
then the dark blue outdoors grew slowly brighter.
You, greeting the evening together with me,
can you hear?

In the beginning we were all new.
Do you remember the novelty of those amazing first times?
Bleeding, the sea at high tide became fresh,
following a breath so light and gasping it seemed about to stop.

I did not realize that I was alive.
Someone out there is listening with ears pricked.
As the door of the sea, come from afar in welcome, opens
crossing through this life, passing through homeless cold,
you, walking the path together with me,
can you hear?

In a Cotton Field

If you follow a mysterious glow like a searchlight one dark night,
you will see a late fall cotton field left for its seeds.
Cotton, bright abstract composition,
multiplying one new moon to a thousand, ten thousand,
your soft, tender approach sheds such great light.

I am a creature busy living, quick on the uptake,
quite unable to make wadded clothes or underwear.
My blood groans if a cold wind blows even a little,
my flesh quails at the least sound of pouring rain,
the family with their shrewd excuses always kept crying
so I had no time to spend at your spacious side.

Growing older, now I reflect that
the best thing in life was warmth.
You whom I have always leaned on in life, so tranquil!
Greediness makes people wilt.
That soft white glow is a wilting cotton field!
If I speak your name, I simply blush for shame.

Cotton! Can I live here by the grace of having met you?
Now, like a legend, I long to relax,
stretch my feet downward, wrap my cold shoulders about.
I want to have again the soft body I had as a child.
You, warmth of all embracing and compassion,
I want to become ageless cotton and grow warm.

My Home

The home of fish is water.
The home of birds is the sky.
My home's the earth, or an empty boat.

Fish sleep in the river's murmur.
Birds sleep in the ring round the moon.
I sleep in a shuddering body chilled by the earth.

In their dreams, fish that cannot once in a lifetime
close their eyes sleep deeply with both eyes closed;
the dreams of sleeping birds fall onto the trees
and wake the sleeping trees in moonless nights.
In the birds' dreams trees are fragrant.

My house is the ear of the earth,
my house where every sound gathers in play
is the sweat of the earth,
receiving the salt dissolved in the water,
anxiety, joy and fevers,
returning from a long stroll
beyond the hidden flesh of blessed symbolism.

My house is earth, a terrestrial boat.
My house, shaking in terrestrial waves of revolt,
is a shaky fishing boat.

Of Gentleness

The little flame inside this empty house
of one who used to speak of gentleness
is today both clearer and more delicate.
This winter morning, as weighty people gather
and quietly cross the river of gentleness,
the cold trees around shake off flurries of snow
and drink in the river's dazzling breath.

You, gentleness that visit me in word and breath,
as I lay here my frozen hand and lower my brow,
beyond the city of noisy folk,
my dear, someone is weeping, shoulders shaking.
Those humble drops of water leave traces on me
and wash the hot flesh of my wandering days.

Twilight glow in the evening that ends my day—
what power the boundless river of gentleness has!
I wished to become strong by that same color.
Why, the blazing clouds are not lonely at all!

THE TRANSLATOR

Brother Anthony of Taizé

Born in Truro, Cornwall (UK), in 1942, Brother Anthony is a member of the monastic Community of Taizé, France. He came to Korea in 1980, and lives in Seoul with other members of the Community. He teaches English literature at Sogang University (Seoul). He has published many volumes of translations of modern Korean poetry, including work by Ku Sang, Sŏ Chŏng-Ju, Ko Un, Chŏn Sang-Pyŏng, Shin Kyŏng-Nim, Kim Su-Yŏng, Lee Si-Yŏng, and others as well as of works of Korean fiction by Yi Mun-Yol and Lee Oyoung. A naturalized Korean citizen, his Korean name is An Sŏnjae.

THE KOREAN VOICES SERIES

EVEN BIRDS LEAVE THE WORLD
SELECTED POEMS OF JI-WOO HWANG
Translated by Won-chun Kim & Christopher Merrill

Ji-woo Hwang's poems describe a life governed by the inescapable reality that all hell can break loose at any time. In the early 1970s, he was arrested and tortured for his anti-government activities, but by the 1980s, he was leading the new wave of deconstructionist poetry which was part of the new "rhetoric of resistance" in Korean literature.

Volume 10   1-893996-45-x/ 104 pages/$14.00 paper

THE DEPTHS OF A CLAM
SELECTED POEMS OF KIM KWANG-KYU
Translated by Brother Anthony of Taize

Born in Seoul in 1941, much of Kim Kwang-kyu 's poetry is sharply critical of the abuses of human dignity caused by corrupt politics and the structural contradictions brought about by the industrialization of society. His essential concern is with the value of each individual and his struggle is to enable people to realize more clearly the social and cultural forces that today threaten their humanity.

Volume 9   1-893996-43-3/160 pages/$16.00 paper

ECHOING SONG
CONTEMPORARY KOREAN WOMEN POETS
Edited by Peter H. Lee

This first anthology of modern Korean women's poetry in either Korean or English demonstrates the originality and variety of the twenty poets whose work is presented: Yi Hyangji, No Hyuangnim, Ch'on Yanghui, Kang Ungyo, Mun Chonghui, Yi Kyongnim, Ko Chonghui, Ch'oe Sungja, Kim Sunghui, Kim Chngnam, Yi Chinmyong, Kim Hesun, No Hyegyong, Hwang Insuk, Chong Hwajinm, Yi Younju, Yi Sanghui, Pak Sowon, Ho Sugyong, and Na Huidok.

Volume 8   1-893996-35-2/304 pages/$18.00 paper

AMONG THE FLOWERING REEDS

CLASSIC KOREAN POEMS IN CHINESE

Edited and translated by Kim Jong-gil

The bulk of the Korean poetic tradition and legacy up until the 17th Century was written in Chinese. This anthology includes 100 poems spanning over 1000 years of poetry introducing this important tradition to the English-speaking audience. "Anyone interested in tasting classical Korean poetry... cannot do better than to start with this collection." — *Multicultural Review*

Volume 7   1-893996-54-9/152 pages/$16.00 paper

BROTHER ENEMY

POEMS OF THE KOREAN WAR

Edited and translated by Suh Ji-moon

The poems in this collection reflect the reality of a country torn apart by war and political ideologies. The work of twenty-one poets, male and female, North and South Korean appear in this landmark anthology.

Volume 6   1-893996-20-4/176 pages/$16.00 paper

SHRAPNEL AND OTHER STORIES

SELECTED STORIES OF DONG-HA LEE

Translated by Hyun-jae Yee Sallee

These stories by one of Korea's most revered storytellers reflect poignantly on the everyday lives of people who find it nearly impossible to cope with the progress that is inexorably wiping out the last vestiges of the Korea they loved and knew. "Stark, challenging, memorable: the work of a superb literary talent." —*Kirkus Reviews*

Volume 5   1-893996-53-0/176 pages/$16.00 paper

Strong Winds At Mishi Pass

Poems by Tong-gyu Hwang

Translated by Seong-Kon Kim & Dennis Maloney

One of the most important poets in contemporary South Korean literature, this volume draws work from three of Hwang's books.. "Paradox and mystery rest comfortably side by side in these reflective poems... Hwang's quiet discoveries...keep pulling me back...for insights as strong as any elixir." —*Pacific Reader*

Volume 4   1-893996-10-7/118 pages/$15.00 paper

A Sketch of the Fading Sun

Stories of Wan-suh Park

Translated by Hyun-jae Yee Sallee

Wan-suh Park delves into the many issues facing women in contemporary Korean society, including the desire for sexual and reproductive freedom, a redefinition of familial expectations, and the struggle for economic independence. "[A] gritty, elegiac collection... Park masterfully explains life in a society in which oppression is never far from hand." — *Choice*

Volume 3   1-877727-93-8/200 pages/$15.00 paper

Heart's Agony

Selected Poems of Chiha Kim

Translated by Won-Chun Kim and James Han

Chiha Kim, first imprisoned in 1964 and sentenced to death in 1974 for writing poetry that provoked the government of Chunghee Park, won the Lotus Prize in 1975. *Heart's Agony* gathers poetry from all eight volumes of his work. "Kim Chiha is a virtuoso, entertaining as well as brilliant." — *World Literature Today*

Volume 2   1-877727-84-9/128 pages/$14.00 paper

THE SNOWY ROAD
AN ANTHOLOGY OF KOREAN FICTION
Translated by Hyun-jae Yee Sallee

This anthology of Korean fiction presents work by winners of the Korean People's Literary Award, including Yean-hee Chung, Ick-suh Yo, Bum-shin Park, Jung-rae Cho, Chung-joon Yee, and Wan-suh Park. The stories offer insight into the lives of ordinary Korean people and the impact of war on their lives. "Wan-suh Park's portrait of a woman seeking... to resolve an inner conflict... is both gentle and perceptive." —*Publisher's Weekly*

Volume 1   1-877727-19-9/168 pages/$12.00 paper

ALSO AVAILABLE

BECAUSE OF THE RAIN
KOREAN ZEN POEMS
Translated by Christopher Merrill & Won-Chun Kim

This selection of Korean Zen poems, spanning twelve centuries, distills the essence of Korean Buddhism. The poets range from Great Master Wonhyo (617–686), the founder of Korean Buddhism, to Choeui Eusoon (1786–1866), a hermit-monk whose poems address the monk's primary goal of seeking enlightenment.

Companions for the Journeyi Series, Volume 10   1-893996-44-1/96 pages/$14.00 paper